The Startup Visa

The Startup Visa:

Key to Job Growth and Economic Prosperity in America

By Tahmina Watson

Edited by Lornet Turnbull

Ebook ISBN: 978-1-78301-697-6

Paperback ISBN: 978-1-78301-696-9

Dedicated to my mother who had a vision for me from the day I was born, to my husband who helped make that vision become reality, and to my daughters who inspire me every day.

Table of Contents

Foreword
By Vivek Wadhwa

The American Dream I knew is losing its luster. Restrictive U.S. immigration policies and the rise of economies of other countries are driving talent elsewhere.

When I immigrated here, America was the greatest land of opportunity for technology entrepreneurs. Standouts in science, engineering, technology and mathematics research flocked here, too. Now they can't get visas. Even as the American economy flounders, advances in technology are making an American reinvention possible. More than ever before, the United States needs immigrant entrepreneurs. These entrepreneurs, however, need America less than ever before. The trend has become so common that it has a name: the reverse brain drain. At almost every entrepreneurship event in Silicon Valley, I meet skilled immigrants on temporary visas who have great ideas, but can't start companies because of their visa restrictions. Visit Bangalore, Shanghai, São Paulo, or any other big city in India, China, or Brazil, and you will find hundreds of innovative startups founded by people trained in U.S. schools and companies.

Not surprisingly, the competition for talent has gotten more intense. Many countries, including Australia, Canada, Chile, China, and

Singapore, recognize the opportunity in attracting entrepreneurs, technologists, and other skilled workers. These countries are offering stipends, labor subsidies for employees, expedited visa processes, and other inducements to bring in startups. As a result of these aggressive recruitment policies, hundreds, if not thousands, of startup companies that might have launched in America are now taking root elsewhere.

To attract that very talent back to the U.S., a Startup Visa is absolutely crucial. And it is the Startup Visa that first connected me to Tahmina. Her immigration law expertise, her first-hand experiences of the various legal obstacles, and her passion for the Startup Visa make her a clear leading authority on the topic and an exceptional advocate for change. No one has yet described the challenges of the current laws and policies as applied to startup founders with such depth and comprehensiveness. Her account of the ineffectiveness of current immigration laws reveals why talented entrepreneurs are actively choosing other countries to found their businesses and why action must be taken if America is to continue to lead the world in innovation. Tahmina's persuasive discussion is a must-read for anyone concerned with the economic future of America.

This book provides valuable policy advice and a guide for entrepreneurs hoping to navigate some of the treacherous waters of the American immigration system.

Vivek Wadhwa

Acknowledgments

There are many people who were instrumental in the creation of this labor of love, proving that it takes a village to conjure up a book.

This book would not be possible were it not for my immensely loving, supportive and encouraging husband, Tom Watson. A patent attorney and partner at his own law firm Amin, Turocy and Watson LLP, Tom is a devoted husband to me, father to our two daughters, and a savior of all of my technology problems. (Yes, I have called him to solve the printer problem when it was, in fact, simply unplugged.)

A genius in his own right, Tom listens to all my passionate immigration arguments, even when I can tell it makes no sense to him. He prints pages of random, irrelevant statutes and bills for me at ungodly hours of the night, supports everything I do unconditionally, and even encourages this crazy passion I have to bring about change.

This book had its inception during a conversation with my client and friend, Mbwana Alliy, founder and managing partner of Savannah Fund, one of the first venture capital firms helping startups in Africa.

As someone who understands the intricate issues related to startups and the depth of my passion and legal knowledge for a Startup Visa, I will be forever grateful for his ideas and encouragement.

I must also thank my Startup Visa cohorts who constantly inspire, motivate and educate me. Craig Montuori, whom I have referred to as Magic Genie, has a wealth of knowledge and connections on anything about startups and related law and policy. Munly Leong, a serial entrepreneur, whose unique entrepreneurial perspective brings an important element to the Startup Visa debate. Jason Wiens, policy director at the Ewing Marion Kauffman Foundation and former deputy legislative director to Sen. Jerry Moran, R-Kansas.

I want to thank Sen. Moran and his legislative director, Mark Colwell, for consistently championing the Startup Act. I have no doubt their tireless efforts will lead to a Startup Visa someday.

I also want to thank some of my colleagues and friends who have been inspirational – Heather Redman, vice president of operations and general counsel of Indix and former general counsel to Getty Images, Inc., who is committed to finding a solution for startup founders. Smeeta Hirani, my dear friend and a writer who helped me understand a little bit about the world of writing. Nicole Hay for being my first book reviewer. My colleagues at the American Immigration Lawyers Association, (AILA), who are constantly fighting for immigration reform and the rights of immigrants. Many of them are good friends, without whom I would find it hard to practice law. I'm especially grateful for the friendships of Belle Woods and Michele Carney who have been mentors in helping me hone my written advocacy skills.

I thank my team at Watson Immigration Law, and especially Silviya Borroff, Jacqui Starr and Nicole Lockett, without whom I would not be able to spend the time I do arguing passionately for reform. They are my reviewers, editors, devil's advocates and fellow debaters on immigration policy matters that come up in the office.

A huge thanks to Fiona McKinnon, my friend and colleague at Watson Immigration Law. For years, she has been my de facto editor of many of the articles appearing in this book, my blog and other publications. Thanks to Jenn Morgan and her team at Radically Distinct, particularly Trudi Jo Davis, whose tremendous help made this book become reality.

My profuse gratitude and thanks to my editor, Lornet Turnbull, without whom this book would simply not be complete. She miraculously appeared just when I needed her most. As a former immigration reporter at *The Seattle Times*, she brings her immigration knowledge and journalism skills to help bring to life the vision and message I wanted to send in this book. I will be forever grateful.

And finally, I want to thank my clients – all of them – for allowing me the privilege of helping with some of the most important issues of their lives. I want to specifically thank my entrepreneur clients who constantly teach me about dedication and passion, about the world of startups, and who inspire and motivate me every day to advocate for change so they can continue to change the world.

Thank you.

Preface

When I founded Watson Immigration Law in 2009, I began to notice a troubling pattern: ambitious young immigrants, eager to start their own businesses, were routinely stymied by a backlog in the system tasked with granting legal permanent residency – green cards – to foreign-born workers in the U.S. Waiting for these visas to become available left many of these workers stuck right where they were – chained to an employer and unable to break out on their own to pursue their innovative ideas. Our immigration system was failing them, falling short of its potential to retain promising immigrant entrepreneurs.

The first Startup Visa Act, intended to break this logjam, was introduced in 2010. The bipartisan measure was recognition by some in Congress of the critical need for a specialty visa that would help retain foreign talent, create jobs and grow the U.S. economy. It never passed. Each year, the need for it grows more urgent. My passion for a breakthrough is matched only by increasing frustration as I've watched Congress, year after year, fail to pass legislation to address this problem.

This book is an outgrowth of a blog I began writing in 2008, along with other articles on immigration. It draws on my experiences as an immigrant, a lawyer and an entrepreneur – and those of my clients – to help demonstrate and offer perspective on why the need for this visa is so critical now.

My hope is it will help law and policy makers, as well as anyone else who wants to understand not only what is happening on the ground but why talented people, educated in our country, are not staying. And I also hope that it will enable a more informed startup community to become better advocates for change.

Introduction

C hange through technology has a powerful impact. Technology has revolutionized the way we work, plan travel, buy houses, study, conduct research, explore the world, cook and clean, buy consumer goods, get our news, watch television, communicate in real time from one end of the globe to another, listen to music and even buy our groceries.

We have wearable technology, which only promises to become more sophisticated with time. You can now print complicated medical devices – even houses – on a 3D printer. Vivek Wadhwa, an academic and entrepreneur,[1] and author of the book, *The Immigrant Exodus-Why America is Losing the Global Race to Capture Entrepreneurial Talent*, recently discussed how our current technological advances are catching up to all that we saw and marveled at in *Star Trek*.[2] By the next generation, travel agents, CDs and even the U.S. Post Office may have joined the Pony Express in the closet of services that technology has made obsolete.

All of these changes, and so many yet to come, are possible because of the ingenuity and creativity of the people behind them – people from every corner of the globe. They are the people who lead the world in innovation and technological advancements. But in order for innovators and entrepreneurs from abroad to bring that talent to the U.S. and apply it here, the U.S. must first provide a straightforward, workable and legal way for them to come here and stay.

Such a path doesn't yet fully exist – but it still can. The Startup Visa would be one such path. It targets bright young minds filled with cutting-edge ideas – those who have figured out how to apply lean, mean businesses practices and use investor cash to grow their businesses from startup to success. Since it was first introduced in Congress in 2010, the bipartisan Startup Visa Act has had several incarnations. And despite broad consensus on its potential benefits to the U.S. economy, the measure has been hobbled repeatedly by political gridlock and has failed to advance. Subsequent measures in Congress to plug this gaping hole in the immigration system have also suffered a similar fate, leaving the U.S. without the necessary tools to attract and retain some of the world's best and brightest entrepreneurs. The most recent attempt to get a measure through Congress was introduced in January 2015 by Sen. Moran, a Kansas Republican, and Sen. Mark Warner, a Virginia Democrat. The bipartisan bill reintroduces the Startup Act and has four other co-sponsors.[3] But just like the versions before it, it too has an uncertain future.

In November 2014, President Obama announced he would use his executive powers to address immigration shortcomings where he could. While the centerpiece of his plan was to make it easier for those living unlawfully in the country, many of its provisions will apply to startup entrepreneurs.

For that, the president should be commended. But it's still not enough. Congressional action is needed to establish a visa to allow us to keep and attract business talent from abroad.

A Startup Visa – which could be applied to high-tech Silicon Valley firms, as well as other industries – will help create new businesses, generate new jobs and raise revenue for local and national economies. Between 1977 and 2005, all net jobs created in the U.S. were by startup firms.[4] They generated 3 million jobs annually between 1992 and 2005.[5] The Ewing Marion Kauffman Foundation, a Kansas City-based non-profit dedicated to advancing educational achievement and entrepreneurial success, predicts that without a Startup Visa, the U.S. will miss the opportunity to create 1.6 million jobs over the next 10 years.[6]

How so? Other countries – Chile, Brazil, Italy, Canada and many others – are starting to recognize what the U.S. has failed to: that immigration has to be part of their nations' economic growth strategy. Not surprisingly, many of these countries are already reaping the benefits of their investments in startup firms.

Each year, the U.S. loses millions in revenue and sends hundreds of thousands of jobs to other countries willing to embrace foreign entrepreneurs – many of them educated and trained at American colleges and universities, sometimes even at U.S. taxpayer expense.

Take for example the case of Kunal Bahl. Bahl, born in India, is a graduate of the Wharton School of Business at the University of Pennsylvania, but was compelled to leave the U.S. because of his immigration status.

In 2010, he founded New Delhi, India-based Snapdeal – dubbed the Amazon of India – which boasts more than 20 million users and employs more than 2,000 people in that country. Snapdeal is on track to reach $1 billion in revenue in 2014-2015.[7] Consider the job creation and revenue generation that India is already seeing from this relatively new company.

In this high-stakes global race to attract and retain the best, the U.S. is gradually losing its edge. Other countries embrace the immigrant entrepreneurs we turn away. Yet we remain the world's most desired location for launching a business – boasting diversity, top schools, enthusiastic investors, a nurturing business climate and a relatively stable political system. America is indeed the Holy Grail for startups.

But we cannot remain complacent. One key to economic prosperity is creating an environment that allows businesses and citizens to thrive. It follows then, that one solution to economic stagnation is not making it harder for foreign entrepreneurs to bring their skills and expertise to the U.S., but rather to welcome and nurture them on our soil – not blindly, but strategically – ultimately reaping the job growth and economic development benefits they will invariably bring.

The way companies bring forth forward-thinking technologies has also evolved. Because technology has become so accessible, entrepreneurs with innovative and workable ideas can start a company anywhere – from their basements, their garages or even their dorm rooms. But as the fledgling company begins to scale up, the need for more money also grows.

Often, these companies rely on funding from investors – from seed funding to series A, B, C and beyond. Those behind the money, such as venture capitalists or angel investors, also play a vital role in bringing high-growth companies to fruition. They, too, see the benefit of attracting entrepreneurial talent from abroad. Nearly half of the top 50 venture-backed companies in America in 2011 had at least one foreign-born founder.[8]

Immigrant founders from top venture-backed firms have created an average of 150 jobs per company in the United States.[9]

As an attorney, I find our current policies outdated and inefficient at moving people through the legal process. It ends up costing the individual, employers and the government unnecessary time and resources – and ultimately costing the country. Laws help us shape our future. And if we want a future of innovation and prosperity, then we need laws to enable it. Immigrant entrepreneurs bring a fresh perspective to business operations by virtue of their diverse experience and a powerful drive to succeed. The Startup Visa will help America maintain its hard-won reputation as an economic powerhouse, a leader among nations. Without it, we risk squandering a great opportunity and resource.

Immigration and Innovation Through History

America is a land of immigrants. Immigrants shaped and fed its democracy, explored its interior, built its infrastructure and honed it, brick by brick and invention by invention, into the world's greatest economy. These immigrants came to this country from everywhere around the globe for its promise of freedom and unlimited potential. They came to build a better life for themselves and their children.

History demonstrates that, despite restrictions placed on immigration since the latter half of the 19th century, economic prosperity and increased immigration go hand in hand. In 1609, Englishman John Rolfe sailed from England to Jamestown, Va., a poor scavenging settlement, where economic desperation had created a cannibalistic colony. Rolfe was the first to figure out how to commercially cultivate a sweet variety of tobacco which became the start of a booming export industry. Jamestown and neighboring towns began to blossom almost overnight.

The industrial revolution of the 19th century is laced with many such stories, as immigrants continued to make a lasting impression on this still-young nation. And nowhere was the industrial growth more apparent than in New York City. Scottish-born Andrew Carnegie came to America with his parents in 1848. The family was dirt poor. An inventor at heart, Carnegie discovered a process for mass producing cheaper steel, which helped transform New York into a vertical city. The city's physical growth brought more businesses and jobs and thus economic prosperity – the foundation of today's modern day New York City.

The story of how Procter & Gamble was founded is particularly captivating. William Procter was an Englishman and candle maker in Cincinnati and James Gamble was an Irishman who was an apprentice soap maker. The two men married sisters Olivia and Elizabeth Norris. Their father-in-law advised them to become business partners and like good sons-in-law, eager to please, they followed his advice. Thus Procter & Gamble was founded in 1837.[10] Today, the Cincinnati-based household products company has 120,000 employees worldwide.

Yet, despite the obvious contributions immigrants have brought, this country, over the generations, has made it increasingly difficult for them to settle here. After gaining independence from Britain, the U.S. Congress declared that any free white person of good moral standing could apply for citizenship after two years' residency. This policy remained intact for nearly a century. But slowly, laws were introduced to restrict immigration, generally on ethnic, moral or health grounds.

By the early 19th Century, America's expansion westward revealed the need for railroads, construction of which was severely hampered by a shortage of workers. Laws were created to allow the immigration of Chinese workers to address the labor shortfall. By 1868, some 4,000 workers – two-thirds of them Chinese – had built the transcontinental railroad.[11] Without them, we would not have the railroad infrastructure that today allows the free movement of goods and services across the United States.

During this period, some famous retailers were established – one of whom would go on to create what is today a world-famous brand. Levi Strauss, born in Germany in 1829, emigrated with his mother and two sisters to the U.S. in 1847. They joined his two brothers in New York, where young Strauss worked in their dry goods business. After becoming a U.S. citizen in 1853, he moved to San Francisco, during the height of the Gold Rush.[12]

He opened a small dry-goods business as his brothers' West Coast agent and there he sold a successful line of fabrics and clothing. His brother-in-law, David Stern, a tailor from Nevada, told Strauss how he could use metal rivets in certain areas of stress on a pair of pants to prevent tear. At that time, miners and other laborers complained their clothes weren't durable enough. Strauss paid for a patent on Levi Strauss & Co., and the blue jeans brand was born in 1873. One hundred and forty two years later, Levi Strauss' jeans are just as popular and fashionable. More importantly, the global company's contribution to the U.S. economy is unquestioned. In 2013, Levi Strauss & Co., reported net income of $229 million, with 16,000 employees and 2,800 company-operated stores worldwide.[13]

Gradually, nativism crept in – primarily for non-Europeans. The Chinese Exclusion Act of 1882 suspended Chinese immigration for 10 years and barred Chinese in the U.S. from obtaining citizenship. And three years later, the law that had permitted the recruitment of unskilled labor was rescinded. By 1917, all Asian immigrants would be barred from the country. This was followed by restrictions, primarily in the form of quotas and literacy tests, designed to reduce immigration.

In the 1920s, in the wake of World War I, piecemeal legislation began to gradually open up immigration, but in smaller, controlled numbers.[14] The strictest controls were placed on people coming from places such as China, Philippines and India. Later, those restrictions were formalized through the Immigration Act of 1924, which limited immigrants to 2 percent of each nationality present in the U.S. in the 1890 U.S. Census. It excluded immigrants from Asia entirely.

During the mid- to latter 1920s, commerce, industrialization and transportation resulted in bigger, sprawling cities where many immigrants had settled. Immigration laws did not see significant changes during this time. However, the Great Depression of 1930, followed by WWII and then the Cold War, put pressure on the economy and society and there was soon consensus that an immigration overhaul was needed.

In 1952, multiple laws that controlled immigration and naturalization in this country at the time, were folded into a single, comprehensive statute which serves as the foundation of today's immigration laws. The Immigration and Nationality Act of 1952 did much to change the immigration landscape, including abolishing the "free white persons" of "good moral character" restrictions.

But more importantly, and for purposes of this discussion, it established a class of immigrants with special, technical skills, who were exempt from any quotas.[15] More than a decade later, Congress passed the Immigration and Nationality Act of 1965, abolishing the national quota system and replacing it with a preference system that focused on immigrant skills and family relationships. It also established a per-country limit, which still exists today.

The 1950s and 1960s gave birth to many renowned companies that today continue to make significant contributions to the U.S. economy. They include retail giants such as Big Lots founded in 1967 by Shol Shenk, a Russian immigrant.

And who hasn't heard of Bose? It is perhaps one of the most recognizable brands of speaker systems. India-born Dr. Amar Bose, an electrical engineer and graduate of Massachusetts Institute of Technology, was its creator. He was inspired to develop the high-end audio system after being disappointed with a stereo system he had purchased. Founded in 1964, Bose is today listed by Forbes as the nation's 167th largest private company with more than 10,000 employees and $2.67 billion in sales.[16]

The next immigration law of note – the Immigration Reform and Control Act (IRCA) of 1986– legalized scores of undocumented people, but also established restrictive provisions for employers who hire them. IRCA also created a new classification of seasonal workers in the agricultural industry.

The following decade saw immigration changes that reflected the economic prosperity and reality of the time. In 1989, laws were enacted to help nurses immigrate to the U.S. to address a widespread shortage. The Immigration Act of 1990 increased total immigration, created separate categories based on family and employment, and instituted diversity visas for countries from which few people were emigrating.

The 1990s were also the start of a high-tech and dot com explosion in this country, with California's Silicon Valley serving as its epicenter. It witnessed the emergence of many of today's top employers. Yahoo! was co-founded in 1994 by Jerry Yang, who was born in Taiwan.

The multinational internet corporation boasted $4.8 billion in revenue in 2013 and more than 12,000 employees worldwide. Paypal's co-founder Elon Musk was also born oversees, in South Africa. He came to the U.S. as a student in the early 1990s. Ebay's founder,

Pierre Omidyar, was born in Paris to Iranian parents and moved to the U.S. when he was a child.

And of course, there's Google. Created in 1997 by Stanford University friends, Larry Page and Sergey Brin, and launched the following year, the company's name is now synonymous with Internet search.[17] Brin was born in Russia in 1973 and immigrated to the U.S. with his family in 1979 to escape Jewish persecution.

Google, Yahoo!, Ebay and Paypal combined supported well over 100,000 American jobs in 2013.[18] Ukrainian native Jan Koum, together with Brian Acton, recently sold their mobile messaging application, Whatsapp, to Facebook for $19 billion.

All of these companies, while U.S. based, are global household names. The Partnership for a New American Economy (PNAE), which advocates "the economic benefits of sensible immigration reform," reports that 40 percent of Fortune 500 companies were founded by immigrants or their children.

The last significant immigration law passed by Congress was the Illegal Immigration Reform and Immigrant Responsibility Act (IIRIRA) of 1996. It focused mainly on enforcement and enacted sanctions for immigration violations, including for employers who fail to comply with regulations. In effect, the new law created harsh measures, though none specifically aimed at entrepreneurs.

Now, with technology advancements affecting every industry, from healthcare to agriculture, it is time to re-think where America wants to be in the next 10, 20 and even 100 years. Archaic laws, remnants of an entirely different time and place, cannot accommodate our need for highly educated and highly skilled workers.

If the status of our laws remain unchanged, we will find ourselves among a mediocre pack. The question is: What kind of country do we want to be in the future?

Around the Globe

Canadä
H-1B Problems?
PIVOT to CANADA
New Start-Up Vis
Low Taxe
immigration.gc.ca/starti

Pivot to Canada. That was the message on a billboard along Highway 101 between San Francisco and San Jose, the heart of Silicon Valley. The May 2013 ad, boasting Canada's brand new Startup Visa, was a bold move to lure American-based entrepreneurs to our neighbor up north. Canada proclaimed this the first visa of its kind in the world. And it was a slap in the face to a dysfunctional American immigration system, seen as unfriendly to startup founders.

Ironically, Canada's Startup Visa legislation is based on language of the Startup Visa Act of 2010, which was introduced and then died in the Congress.

Whereas Canada is up and running in recruiting talented skilled entrepreneurs, the U.S. version has not moved an inch. Bipartisan Startup Visa legislation was again reintroduced in Congress in January 2015. However, with Republicans in full control of both the

House of Representatives and the Senate, it will be interesting to see whether there is a chance of the bill passing.

Meanwhile, under the Canadian Startup Visa, foreign nationals – with funding from a government-approved list of about two dozen Canadian venture capital firms or angel investor groups – can apply for immediate permanent residency. The Canadian law provides 2,750 visas to foreign entrepreneurs for each year of the five-year pilot program.

Each entrepreneur must secure a minimum investment of $200,000 if the investment comes from designated Canadian venture capital funds, or $75,000 if it comes from a designated Canadian angel investor group. Canada issued its first visas to two Ukrainian entrepreneurs in July 2014 and as of January 2015, had issued a total of five. While slow to take off, five years from now it is likely that Canada will see much benefit from the Startup Visa.

Like Canada, other countries are eager to attract entrepreneurs, enticing them with special visas and funding. Between 2012 and 2014, from the Americas to the Asian continent, several countries implemented new policies and programs to bring innovation and job creation within their borders. A prime example is Startup Chile, which was created in 2010. Chile offers a $40,000 grant for seed funding to qualified entrepreneurs from around the world.

The program requires the foreign entrepreneur to teach Chilean youth about business. In addition, the businesses generally hire two or three local citizens. The unique government-funded program has generated much financial growth and job creation and has inspired other positive effects.[19] Brazil recently replicated the model, creating "Startup Brazil."

In a desperate bid to boost employment following an economic meltdown, Ireland also created a Startup Entrepreneur program in April 2012. Its aim is to foster new enterprises, for which the program applicant must have financial backing of no less than €75,000. Approved participants and their immediate families will be allowed to enter Ireland on multi-entry visas and remain there for two years. The program has so far been successful and likely will see more success in the near future. Since its inception about two years ago, 21 visas have been granted.[20]

In 2012, the United Kingdom launched its Tier One Entrepreneur visa, which offers investors permanent residency if they invest £200,000 in a UK business. The program is part of a five-tier, points-based visa system that exists for those trying to immigrate to the UK. Tier 1 visas are aimed at entrepreneurs, investors and the very small number of people who qualify under what's known as the 'exceptional talent' visa category.

The UK also launched Go UK, a business plan competition designed to boost investment in the region. It is open to Australian firms with an interest in expansion into the UK. Successful applicants receive return airfares to London, where they have access to potential business partners, client contacts, business networks and services. In July 2014, that visa became the subject of controversy due to fraudulent applications. Although the rules were tightened, the visa is still available to legitimate entrepreneurs.

Also in 2014, New Zealand and Italy launched their own versions of the Startup Visa. The Netherlands also jumped on board, approving a Startup Visa in December 2014 and launching it in January 2015. Countries with similar programs include Germany, Singapore and South Korea.

Although many of these new Startup Visas have their own limitations, they demonstrate an eagerness by a growing number of countries to embrace foreign entrepreneurs, while the U.S. remains mired in political gridlock. We make it easy for immigrants to acquire the best education here, but then practically force them to go elsewhere to put that knowledge to work. As stated by Vivek Wadhwa, "Gone are the days when the U.S. was the only land of opportunity and when entrepreneurs dreamed of being acquired by a Silicon Valley company. The bigger opportunities now lie in countries such as India, China and Brazil, and their entrepreneurs are becoming confident that they can take on Silicon Valley."[21]

Yet entrepreneurs actually want to be in the U.S. The market is larger and businesses are relatively easy to open. Investors willing to take risks are more accessible. However, without the availability of a Startup Visa, we stand to lose talented people, and the opportunity to remain leaders in innovation and job creation. The American Bar Association, the U.S. Chamber of Commerce and the Partnership for a New American Economy are among the many organizations that back a Startup Visa. Lawmakers from both sides of the aisle also support one. Former New York City Mayor Michael Bloomberg summed it up this way: "When every other country wants the best and the brightest, we're trying to keep them out. It doesn't make a lot of sense... [T]he truth of the matter is we are sending the future overseas. We need people to start companies and create jobs. People that come from overseas are something like ... five times more likely to create jobs than people who are here... So we've got to do something about this."[22]

Square Pegs in Round Holes

Every country wants to be home to the next founder of Facebook, Google or Microsoft. But increasingly, entrepreneurs in the U.S. are finding themselves mired in outdated rules and regulations. One reason is because Congress has failed to act to address this shortcoming in our laws. But another is because, like trying to force square pegs into round holes, our current visa options are not viable for most foreign entrepreneurs. I summarize the various options here and explain why they don't work well for startups.

EB-5 Investor Visa:

The current investor visa program established in 1990 allows for immediate permanent residency for those who: (1) invest $1 million in any business in any part of the U.S. and generate 10 new full-time jobs; or (2) invest $500,000 in a targeted employment area (TEA) and generate 10 new full-time jobs. The law defines a targeted employment area as either rural or an area of high unemployment.

The EB-5 has contributed significantly to the U.S. economy. Investments in FY 2012 alone added more than $3.39 billion to the

U.S. gross domestic product, supported over 42,000 American jobs, and generated over $712 million in federal, state and local tax revenue – all at no cost to the U.S. taxpayer.[23]

However, the EB-5 visa program is a poor fit for boot-strapped, hardworking, talented and creative entrepreneurs, who generally don't have this kind of money at their disposal. This visa is for the investor who is not interested in being the next Google founder, but wants to dump money into a safe and successful project that will allow him or her to fulfill the requirements to obtain a green card.

Incidentally, it is worth noting that Canada scrapped its EB-5 equivalent in 2013 because it was not deemed a job-generator, and was creating inequalities for Canadian citizens. In December 2014, however, it announced plans to launch a brand new program to allow only 50 high-net-worth immigrant investors annually to actually invest in startups, demonstrating that Canada is being creative in finding more ways to attract foreign investment.[24]

E-2 Treaty Investor Visa:

Citizens of countries with which the U.S. maintains a treaty of commerce and navigation – 40 countries to date – can apply for an E-2 visa. It allows entrepreneurs to come to the U.S. with their families, if they have the financial wherewithal to operate a business here. This visa can be issued for up to five years at a time, with no limits on renewal, but on its own can never lead to legal permanent residency for its holders.

Like the EB-5, the E-2 benefits the economy by bringing capital infusion and creating jobs. But it has many limitations.

Because it's a non-immigrant visa, the holder may only reside in the U.S. as long as the business is active and profitable. Furthermore, not all countries maintain the required treaties with the U.S.[25] Therefore, the majority of graduates and high-skilled workers coming from India and mainland China are ineligible for an E-2. I have many clients who are otherwise eligible but cannot benefit from this visa because of their nationalities.

While the law does not specify the investment necessary to obtain an E-2 visa, it does state that a substantial amount of money should be invested.[26] Most immigration lawyers say the rule of thumb is to invest around $100,000 for a successful case, although lesser amounts have also qualified. As with the EB-5, most founders do not have that kind of money to invest in a business.

An additional problem: to qualify for an E-2 visa, an applicant must have at least 51 percent ownership in the business. However, if the ownership structure includes funding from investors, and especially if there are multiple founders, the foreign entrepreneur might see shares dwindle below 51 percent, preventing continued eligibility for this visa.

H-1B Employment Visa:

The H-1B visa is the workhorse of U.S. employment visas, easily the most popular and aimed specifically at skilled professionals who have earned at least a Bachelor's degree. Each year, 65,000 visas are issued to foreign-born people to work in any number of jobs – from computer programmers to high school teachers. An additional 20,000 are granted to those who hold a Master's degree from an American college or university; an unlimited number are granted to researchers, professors and other workers at American colleges, universities and certain research institutes. The H-1B is valid for six years. It is initially granted for three years and can be extended for another three. To extend beyond the initial six years, however, an applicant must have a green card application pending or approved.

While this visa is the most widely used by U.S. employers to fill skilled-worker positions, for entrepreneurs seeking to start companies, it is not a particularly good fit.

Traditionally, the H-1B visa has not been used for the self-employed. However, in August 2011, U.S. Citizenship and Immigration Services (USCIS) announced a policy change to allow entrepreneurs to apply for H-1Bs through their own startup companies.[27] The company itself – not the entrepreneur – must file the petition and there must be evidence that the entrepreneur is an employee of the company. While the policy has seen some success, there are many problems with applying the H-1B to entrepreneurs.

Numerical limitation is the most obvious. The demand for H-1B visas is far greater than the supply. In 2013 and 2014, for example, the cap was reached in just five days. Actually, the number of visas could have been exhausted on the first day the government began accepting applications, but the law requires the window remain open for five days when demand is high.[28]

The total number of applications received in April 2014 was 172,500, more than double the number of visas available. An entrepreneur growing a business cannot afford the uncertainty of such a lottery.

There are other requirements of the H-1B visa that make it inefficient for startups. For example, the company must prove the owner's salary will be at the prevailing wage, defined as the wages and benefits paid to the majority of workers in the largest city in each county. Because technology wages are high, the prevailing wage in that industry is substantial. The typical startup company, struggling during its fledgling years to stay afloat, is not always able financially to accommodate this provision. In addition, USCIS has challenged practically every aspect of such petitions, resulting in denials, even for obviously approvable cases.

Another gaping hole is that the job description of the founder's H-1B position must match the tasks described in the Department of Labor's job library. For example, a computer programmer must perform all the duties of a computer programmer. However, a founder will be wearing many other hats, in addition to computer programming, and therefore a narrow interpretation of the H-1B job description will pose a problem.

L-1 Intra-Company Transferee:

In an era of globalization, the L-1 is an often used visa that allows certain personnel – usually a manager or executive, as well employees with special knowledge – to transfer to the U.S. from a foreign office or an affiliate of a U.S. company. To qualify, the foreign office must be related to the U.S. office with the same or similar ownership and the employee must have worked in that foreign office for at least one of the past three years. The L-1 has been a vehicle for many businesses to establish a presence in the U.S. While I do not represent them, it is likely that the Chinese e-commerce giant, Alibaba, will use this kind of visa to relocate many of its employees to the U.S., possibly including its co-founder, Jack Ma.

The L-1 visa, though, comes with its own unique problems. Requiring foreign and U.S. companies to have a qualifying relationship – as a parent firm with a subsidiary, affiliate or a branch office – is perhaps the most problematic. An entrepreneur seeking to start a new company in the U.S. would most likely not have a foreign affiliate or subsidiary, let alone meet the one-year working requirement.

But beyond that, almost all L-1 visas for new companies have recently faced increased scrutiny for fear of fraud. In 2013, the Department of Homeland Security's Office of Inspector General issued a lengthy report outlining various recommendations that will prompt even more scrutiny of applications.[29] This visa simply does not fit the circumstances of most startup founders.

O-1 Extraordinary Ability

The O-1 visa, dubbed the genius visa, is reserved for those who can prove they are at the top echelon of their profession and are indeed extraordinary. Frequently used by celebrities, such as British journalist Piers Morgan who replaced Larry King on CNN in 2010, this temporary work visa is being used more often for high-tech entrepreneurs. Some requirements include proof the applicant has acquired national or international acclaim, mention in the media, a significant contribution in their field – for example, finding the cure for cancer. A full list can be found at 8 CFR §214.2(o).

However, the standard for meeting such a high burden of proof is extremely difficult, and most new entrepreneurs cannot do so for several reasons. Many will be graduating from college so they will not have had the career or life experiences to reach the highest levels of their profession.

In other circumstances, they may have had long careers at companies where they focused on a special service or product. And while they may have expertise in that one thing, they will not have had the opportunity to develop their careers in the way the O visa mandates. Thus, it is not always appropriate for entrepreneurs.

EB-1 Extraordinary Ability

While the O-1 is only a temporary work visa, the EB-1 visa is for permanent residency and can lead to a green card. The requirements mirror those of the O visa. And for the same reasons, it also is not a good fit for entrepreneurs. While it can be used when the startup founder has received much public acknowledgment for raising large sums of money and creating many jobs, that often is still not enough to meet the requirements for this visa.

National Interest Waiver

At the same time it announced the self-employed H-1B policy change in 2011, USCIS also unveiled a plan to broaden the scope of something known as the National Interest Waiver (NIW) that would help entrepreneurs file petitions for legal permanent residency.[30] The NIW is an application process to obtain a green card in the U.S. without the need for a family petition or offer of employment. It has no legal definition. USCIS relies on a 1998 Administrative Appeals Office precedent decision setting forth a three-pronged test for evaluating requests for it.[31] First, the area of work must be of substantial intrinsic merit. Second, the work must benefit the nation as a whole. And finally, the work must have the potential to be in the national interest of the United States. In other words, the NIW allows an immigrant to directly obtain a green card simply because his or her work is in the national interest. It is typically used by medical researchers. It's a high bar indeed.

Entrepreneurs welcomed this policy adjustment when it was made. USCIS made the change because the process currently in place to petition for an employment-based green card for H-1B workers cannot be applied to the self-employed. Why? Under current law, traditional employers petitioning for a green card for their immigrant employees must demonstrate a good-faith effort to first recruit American workers. Obviously, someone starting his or her own business can't do that.

However, to date, there are few NIW success stories for entrepreneurs. In a recent inquiry made with USCIS, I was informed there is no way to identify such cases. Nevertheless, the biggest problem in these petitions is more fundamental: whether entrepreneurs can prove their ventures will benefit the nation. Depending on the type of business and industry, typical startup companies that generate jobs locally may not be able to meet the waiver's requirement that the benefit be national in scope.

An additional problem with the NIW is that the waiting time for obtaining a green card through this path can be long. It falls within a visa-granting category where the wait can be decades for citizens of India, China, Mexico and the Philippines. Therefore, a large number of people will not be able to benefit from the rule change as was intended.

* * *

Each of the above visas work well for certain cases and they've resulted in many foreigners being able to stay in the U.S., work here and in some cases start businesses. But those instances are too few and the process is too tortured. These visas are ill-suited for the immigrant who wants to start and grow a new business and, in some instances, secure funding from investors.

What's more, none takes into consideration that increasingly, in an era of high-speed Internet when technology is cheap and easy to access, someone with a brilliant idea doesn't always need a significant amount of money to get a startup off the ground. Facebook and Google are examples of such success, started by founders during college and graduate school, respectively. Immigration policies must reflect that, too.

Pity the Startup Founder

O n January 8, 2010, Donald Neufeld, associate director of
service center operations of USCIS, issued a memo imposing
drastic restrictions on employment-based visa petitions.[32] His
action was triggered by a 2008 USCIS report, *H-1B Benefit Fraud and
Compliance Assessment*, which found that 13 percent of these petitions
filed by employers were fraudulent. It flagged as a fraud indicator,
those employers with fewer than 25 employees and less than $10
million in gross revenue. The study also found a lack of adherence to
the job descriptions outlined in Department of Labor guidelines. In
seeking to address these problems, Neufeld imposed strict burdens
on proving an employer-employee relationship for H-1B petitions,
namely that the employer has a right to hire and fire the employee
and that it controls his or her work. The 15-page fraud report
affected all employers – big and small.

Coming on the heels of what in the industry has become known as
the Neufeld Memo, was that set of guidelines from the USCIS that,
for the first time, allowed startup founders to apply for H-1B visas.
Even sole proprietors could apply.

But while initially applauded, the challenge of these changes, when
taken together, was immediately obvious. The guidelines were

predicated upon the Neufeld memo and required startup companies applying for H-1B visas to produce evidence that the founder's employment was controlled by the company. A board of directors could be sufficient to prove such control element.

Proving that the employer controls the work of the employee when the founder is both employer and employee can be tricky. The USCIS expects an onerous amount of corporate documentation, including articles of incorporation, board meeting minutes, shareholder agreements, stock ledgers, etc. This extreme burden often results in denial of the case.

The case of one client, whose real name, like all others I mention in this chapter, has been changed to protect his identity, illustrates the problem. Todd Leahry, a Canadian citizen, is co-founder of a company that employs seven full-time American workers and has helped create several indirect jobs by virtue of those who use and sell his product. Todd, his U.S.-born partner and their company have garnered wide praise from throughout the tech industry. In early 2011, when his company made the initial filing for his H-1B visa, the Neufeld Memo was in play, but the USCIS self-employment guidelines had not yet been released. So it wasn't necessary for Todd to disclose that he was part owner of the company; policy did not require it. The employer-employee relationship still applied and in Todd's case, was proven with relevant documents.

When Todd sought to extend his H-1B two years later, he filed a petition just like the first one, without specific mention of ownership. However, by then, the self-employment guidelines were in force and they were predicated upon meeting the Neufeld Memo requirements. What that meant was that Todd's company had to prove that it controlled his employment.

Following a series of requests for further evidence during the renewal of his visa, the final request centered on the relationship between Todd and his firm. The USCIS believed that it was discovering for the first time that Todd was a co-founder of his company. Suddenly, Todd faced the real possibility of having to leave the U.S., because the government believed he may have been trying to hide his relationship with his company, which was not the case at all. Before the USCIS issued its self-employment guidelines, ownership interest in a firm did not have to be specifically disclosed. It was at this stage I was brought in to help file the response.

It was a privilege to help my client win this case. As a team, we brainstormed the type of documentation he would be able to provide. We decided to give the government many internal, otherwise confidential documents, to demonstrate he was always given direction in his work and he was not the decision maker. We submitted emails, client contracts, employee information, payroll evidence, references and much more. It was a burdensome and challenging request.

It illustrates how startups are sometimes treated in the H-1B context and the difficulties that can arise. By their very nature, startup companies operate leanly. Their founders often work around the clock to ensure their enterprises are successful – that employees are properly supervised and clients are happy.

But rather than using his energy to build the business, Todd had to spend a great deal of time anxious and worried about providing enough of the right kind of information to respond to the government.

During this period, my client suffered losses both emotionally and financially. As a result, his business, partners, employees, and clients were all put in limbo. He faced the real possibility of having to uproot his wife and family from the U.S. – a proposition that he knew would be so upsetting to his wife, he kept it a secret from her for as long as he could.

It makes no sense to create an environment of inefficiency at a crucial time when an entrepreneur is trying to get his business off the ground. One should not have to feel defensive for founding a company; it should be a source of pride. Luckily, in Todd's case, we were able to successfully demonstrate that his employment was controlled by his company. But many founders are not so lucky. Too many end up cut off from the companies they helped to create by our policies and laws, which are often disconnected from the demands of today's modern world where globalization has made nations, economies and people more connected than ever.

While Todd was able to eventually continue to work for his firm with an H-1B visa, Kumar Patel, a citizen of India, was not as lucky. Kumar had come to the U.S. as a student almost 20 years earlier, completed his Bachelor's and Master's degrees in engineering, and went on to work at some of the top Fortune 500 companies in the country, including Microsoft. Microsoft had petitioned for a green card on his behalf. However, the wait for a green card to become available for someone from India currently exceeds 15 years[33] and sadly, Kumar is still waiting. In the meantime, he continues to nurture ideas for creating products that could literally change people's lives. He wants to start his own company, but can't because he's stuck in a holding pattern waiting for a green card.

First, there is no suitable visa for him to start his own company, other than the self-employed H-1B, which is too risky for him to try. Second, there is no mechanism to transfer his pending green card application to a startup company. So, he continues his daily life working at Microsoft but dreaming of the day he can create his own company. Sadly, because of his age, he may not get the opportunity to do so in his lifetime.

Some would-be entrepreneurs end up becoming so frustrated, they give up and return home, where they try to develop there, what they are unable to here. That was the case with Jamal Jay, a bright and talented young man from India. Upon graduation from a U.S. college, Jamal worked under an H-1B visa for Microsoft, which diligently applied for his green card. Like Kumar, Jamal also became a victim to the waiting game. He transferred his H-1B to another company, but that did not address his desire to open his own company.

In addition to his own frustrations, his wife – a professional woman in her own right – was not allowed to work. H-4 visas, available to the spouses of H-1B workers, have not, by law, been permitted to work in this country. That is scheduled to change under new policies instituted by President Obama's Executive Action.

These mounting frustrations compelled the couple recently to return to India, where Jamal intends to launch his startup. He may or may not return to the U.S. But what a shame that we are educating bright, promising young people who end up taking their education and training somewhere else?

And it's not just people from the Asian continent, either. Joey Grayson is a Canadian citizen who also worked at Microsoft on an H-1B visa before teaming up with friends to launch a startup. To be clear, Joey did not have a huge stake in this company – a negligible 2 percent.

He resigned from Microsoft and returned to Canada around the time they were trying to get the business started. Since employment visas are employer specific, we needed to find an option that would allow the new company to sponsor Joey so he could return to the U.S. The question was how to get his visa through a startup firm, in which he owns some stock.

Citizens of Canada are eligible to apply for what's known as a Treaty NAFTA (TN) visa, approval for which can be relatively quick and easy if all the requirements are met. Generally, the TN visa applicant cannot be self-employed. In this case, Joey's company was too new and USCIS viewed it with suspicion. So Joey's initial application was denied. He was now stuck in Canada and separated from the business. After a few months, with a little revenue stream and more substantial finances in the business, the TN was approved – but for only a year, which is not much time.

The business was gaining ground and growing stronger in a short period of time, but Joey's visa timeline was coming to an end. At this time, around 2009, self-employed H-1Bs were not yet specifically allowed but the business also needed more sustainable revenue for a successful application, as a prevailing wage is the foundation of the petition. The business was poised to receive funding from investors and Joey's immigration status was crucial to securing that investment. In the end, he married his long-term girlfriend – a U.S. citizen – which solved his immigration problem. While Joey was lucky to have found the love of his life, matrimony is not an option for everyone.

Since Congress had proven incapable of enacting new legislation, the USCIS, under the leadership of then-Director of USCIS Alejandro Mayorkas, created a new initiative in 2012 called the Entrepreneur in Residence (EIR) program. Its aim was to help immigrant entrepreneurs – and they welcomed it. The program brings together immigration adjudication officers and startup experts with fresh ideas for working within the current legal framework.[34] Officers are trained in modern-day entrepreneurial issues, allowing them to make more informed decisions. This training is key, as it takes into account USCIS' new policy changes that allowed self-employed H-1Bs and NIW for entrepreneurs. In essence, the EIR team at USCIS is trained to adjudicate all entrepreneur cases with a keen understanding of how startups operate.

For some entrepreneurs, the addition of the EIR team, together with the new, updated policy guidance, was a reprieve – albeit temporary. A Canadian citizen born in Korea, Alan Leffert was a genius in his own right. He, too, worked at Microsoft and resigned to start his own company. He wanted to change the way certain high-end consumer products sold online. When the USCIS allowed self-employed H-1Bs, he became a program pioneer. He had to prove his business partner was going to control his work and have the ability to hire or fire him. Documentation to that effect had to be created, including for Alan to relinquish voting rights in the business. He was lucky enough to get an H-1B with his new company in a matter of days, thanks in part to the EIR officers' understanding of startups. While he, his partner and venture capitalists invested heavily in the company, the fast-growing startup was still having cash flow problems, common for startups that are scaling up. Maintaining the terms of his H-1B status – that he be paid a prevailing wage of $100,000 a year – was a real struggle. It's one of many reasons the H-1B is not well suited for startups. Until the firm's revenue stream stabilizes, finances are always tight. So Alan is not in an ideal situation to grow his company.

What's more, he needs permanent residency to ensure investors can rely on him being able to continue running it. His H-1B timeline is limited and his green card options are limited because he has ownership in his company.

As discussed before, the traditional process of parlaying an H-1B visa into a green card – also known as the permanent labor certification application – works against those with ownership interests in a company. As a result, when USCIS established a new policy in August 2011, it allowed entrepreneurs to utilize the National Interest Waiver visa – to prove their work will have a national impact – in order to apply for green cards.

It was the most practical and sensible option for Alan, yet, there is no certainty his petition will be approved. While his company might well be able to prove this new method of online sales does indeed have broad, national influence, it takes time for a startup to become established and spread its business impact. Alan's business has 15 full-time employees. While job creation is what the national interest waiver for entrepreneurs generally seeks, the arguments for national intrinsic merit and national scope – the standards used – have a very high bar. So, Alan's situation is precarious to say the least and he may be compelled to leave the U.S.

Another temporary success story of the EIR program is Norman Romanio, another Canadian citizen. Norman was selected to participate in Techstars Seattle, a 13-week mentorship-driven program to accelerate startup companies. After he graduated in 2008, he obtained an H-1B visa through his company.

This was before the Neufeld Memo. Norman was one of several co-founders of the company, but not its CEO. Prior to the 2011 self-employment policy change, ownership did not have to be disclosed as such, especially when there was another person at the company to sign the H-1B application forms. I believe that worked in his favor then.

Two years later, the most successful of his products and assets were acquired by a large company, likely for several million dollars. This is the dream of any startup founder. As part of the deal, Norman worked for the company that acquired the product. In fact, thanks to his product, the acquiring company was named one of the fastest-growing tech companies in New York. It generated millions of dollars in revenue and created almost 300 jobs.

By 2013, however, Norman was coming to the end of his term with the acquiring company and decided to revive the original firm that started it all.

USCIS is generally cautious of fraud and conducts thorough checks of companies' documentation to verify authenticity and ensure employers can afford to pay prevailing wage to their H-1B employees. The trouble for Norman was that the initial company had been dormant for some time, with no financial activity. Typically, this is a death knell for an H-1B petition. I came into the picture at this stage to assess how we could re-apply for the H-1B through a company unlikely to pass the fraud smell-test.

After assessing the conditions, I decided to trust the EIR program and its officers to recognize a genius startup founder. Instead of hiding the dormancy of the company, which would come out later anyway and seem even more suspicious, I decided to lay all the cards on the table.

I explained how talented Norman is, describing the revenue he has generated so far and the jobs he helped create in America. I explained that given the chance again, Norman would be able replicate the model and continue to be an asset in the U.S. The trust worked and an EIR startup-trained adjudicator approved the case.

But now Norman faces the green card issue. We will apply for the NIW and he may well be successful. Or not. The unpredictability and the inconsistency of adjudicating these cases and the lack of policy guidance – even with EIR officers involved – leave him in a precarious situation. If his case is denied, he would have to return to Canada. Whose loss would that be?

For each of the above people, a Startup Visa would have been ideal. Visa requirements would have set forth guidelines for things like jobs created, revenue generated and funds raised. The founders would have been freed up to run their businesses. In the current economic race to the top, does the U.S. really want to lose such talented people?

Legislative History

While the story of the entrepreneurial immigrant is not new, it wasn't until 2010 that lawmakers finally introduced a bill in Congress to create a path specifically designed for them to obtain legal permanent status here. Since then, lawmakers have introduced several major bills authorizing a Startup Visa program. None has passed.

Former Sens. John Kerry, D-Mass., and Richard Lugar, R-Ind., introduced the first one, S. 3029, with the aim of driving job creation and increasing America's global competitiveness. It would allow immigrant entrepreneurs to receive a two-year conditional immigrant visa if they could show that a qualified American investor was willing to dedicate a significant sum – a minimum of $250,000 – to the immigrant's startup venture and create a certain number of jobs. It would also create a new visa category for immigrant entrepreneurs, called EB-6, borrowing from the current EB-5 visa category, which permits foreign nationals who invest at least $1 million in a U.S. project, thereby creating 10 jobs, to obtain a green card. Although more than 160 venture capitalists from across the country endorsed the senators' proposal, the legislation never made it out of the Senate Judiciary Committee, where it died at the end of the 111th Congress.

Another attempt to enact Startup legislation came the following year, when Sens. Lugar and Kerry, along with Sen. Mark Udall, a Democrat from Colorado, reintroduced the legislation. The Startup Visa Act of 2011, S. 565, was an expanded version of the original. In addition to many key provisions spelled out in the original bill, this new version sought to broaden the potential pool of eligible immigrants to include those already here on H-1B visas, as well as entrepreneurs living outside the U.S. It also established new visa options for foreign entrepreneurs already living in the U.S. on E-2 visas as well as for entrepreneurs living abroad, setting forth conditions for each that included investment in their company, revenue generation and job creation. Unfortunately, this bill, too, never made it out of the Judiciary Committee.

In May 2012, Startup Act 2.0 was introduced by Sen. Jerry Moran, R-Kan. The legislation, S. 3217, called for a STEM visa to allow graduates in the fields of science, technology, engineering and math, to stay in the U.S. and start their own companies. The bill also proposed an entrepreneur visa and elimination of per-country caps for employment-based immigration. It died shortly after introduction.

In February the following year, Moran again, along with Sens. Mark Warner, D-Va., Chris Coons, D-Del., and Roy Blunt, R-Mo., introduced the Startup Act 3.0, S. 310, to create both an entrepreneur and a STEM visa. The Entrepreneur Visa would allow entrepreneurs to enter and stay in the country, launch businesses and create jobs. The STEM Visa would allow U.S.-educated foreign students, with an advance degree in any STEM field, to receive a green card. But this bill also stalled. It is this same bill that was reintroduced in January 2015 as The Startup Act, S.181.

Senate Bill 744:

Amid great anticipation and much fanfare, a bipartisan comprehensive immigration reform measure – the Border Security, Economic Opportunity and Immigration Modernization Act – was introduced in the Senate in April 2013. The centerpiece of the massive bill, and perhaps its most controversial component, sought to create a legal path for those in the country unlawfully.

But it seemed to have something for everyone – including entrepreneurs. The bill incorporated many of the provisions of Startup Act 3.0, including two new immigrant and non-immigrant visa categories for entrepreneurs.

The bill established requirements for this visa, called Invest Visa, based on jobs created and either funds raised from investors or revenue generated by the company. It also granted a preference to STEM graduates. On the following page is a diagram summarizing the terms of the bill.

The Invest Visa provisions in the bill were seen as a creative solution to allow entrepreneurs to test their models before applying for green cards. The visa would be applicable to all industries, not just technology. I believe it is a good idea to have both temporary and permanent visa options as it would allow the government to assess the success of the business during the temporary visa stage before granting permanent residency.

In the end, after much debate and analysis from nearly every sector, S. 744 passed the Democrat-controlled Senate in June 2013 – a historic win given that no immigration bill had passed that chamber in decades. However, it died in the Republican-controlled House.

Invest Visa
S. 744: Subtitle H– Investing in New Ventures, Entrepreneurial Startups and Technologies

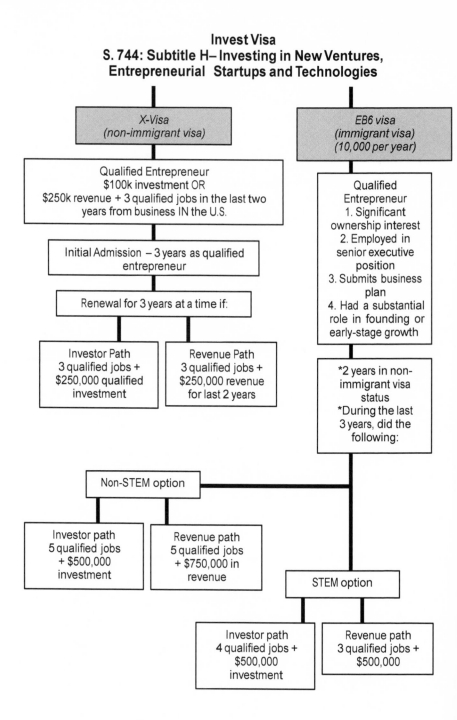

X-Visa
(non-immigrant visa)

Qualified Entrepreneur
$100k investment OR
$250k revenue + 3 qualified jobs in the last two years from business IN the U.S.

Initial Admission – 3 years as qualified entrepreneur

Renewal for 3 years at a time if:

Investor Path
3 qualified jobs +
$250,000 qualified investment

Revenue Path
3 qualified jobs +
$250,000 revenue for last 2 years

Non-STEM option

Investor path
5 qualified jobs
+ $500,000 investment

Revenue path
5 qualified jobs
+ $750,000 in revenue

EB6 visa
(immigrant visa)
(10,000 per year)

Qualified Entrepreneur
1. Significant ownership interest
2. Employed in senior executive position
3. Submits business plan
4. Had a substantial role in founding or early-stage growth

*2 years in non-immigrant visa status
*During the last 3 years, did the following:

STEM option

Investor path
4 qualified jobs +
$500,000 investment

Revenue path
3 qualified jobs +
$500,000

The SKILLS Visa Act:

About the same time the Senate was debating S. 744, another startup bill was introduced in the House. H.R. 2131 – the Supplying Knowledge-based Immigrants and Lifting Levels of STEM Visas Act or SKILLS Visa Act, sponsored by Rep. Darrell Issa, R-Calif.[35] Unlike the measure in the Senate, Issa's bill did not have much support. Rep. Zoe Lofgren, D-Calif., said the bill takes a "zero sum approach" to high-skilled immigration reform and "gives to some by only taking away from others."[36] It was reported out of the House Judiciary Committee in July 2013 and that is where it remains.

H.R. 2131 includes provisions for a Startup Visa, called the "Entrepreneur Visa" or EB-8 – a two-pronged instrument, aimed on one hand at entrepreneurs with venture capital backing and on the other at foreigners already in the country on an E-2 Treaty Investor visa.

On the following page is a chart of the bill's proposed provisions.

While the bill attempts to address the lack of a visa for entrepreneurs, the provisions will not accomplish the intended goal. For one thing it establishes financial thresholds that are way too high. It's nearly impossible for people to secure funding from a U.S. investor without already being in the U.S. And even if they can obtain the initial funding, it is virtually impossible for the majority of people to secure an additional $1 million in funding or revenue generation in only two years. A venture capital firm or angel investor, who has already invested in the company, will no doubt be vested in its success. But such success can take time to observe and nurture. Without making an assessment of the ongoing business needs, it is unlikely that an investor will put an additional $1 million into the business.

Entrepreneur Visa
SKILLS Visa Act (HR 2131)

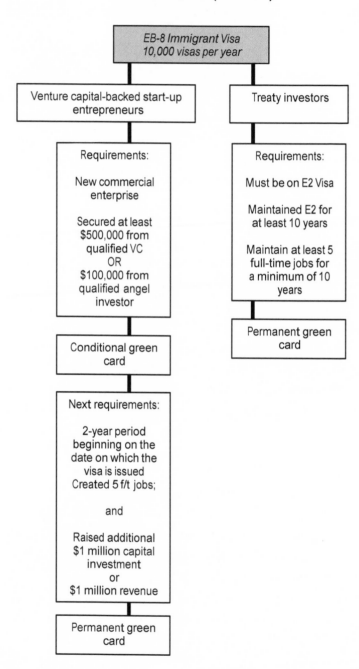

EB-8 Immigrant Visa
10,000 visas per year

Venture capital-backed start-up entrepreneurs

Requirements:

New commercial enterprise

Secured at least $500,000 from qualified VC
OR
$100,000 from qualified angel investor

Conditional green card

Next requirements:

2-year period beginning on the date on which the visa is issued
Created 5 f/t jobs;

and

Raised additional $1 million capital investment
or
$1 million revenue

Permanent green card

Treaty investors

Requirements:

Must be on E2 Visa

Maintained E2 for at least 10 years

Maintain at least 5 full-time jobs for a minimum of 10 years

Permanent green card

Another fault of this legislation is regarding those who can take advantage of the second prong, where one must already be in the U.S. on an E-2 visa to apply. As a result, only a small pool of people might be able to qualify.

These provisions are too stringent and will not be usable if passed. Thus, it will give the appearance of a startup visa, but in reality almost no one will be able to utilize it.

In October 2013, a Democratic coalition in the House, led by Rep. Joe Garcia, D-Fla., introduced H.R.15, the Border Security, Economic Opportunity, and Immigration Modernization Act of 2013. I was proud that my home-state Congresswoman, Suzan Delbene, D-Wash., cosponsored the bill and took a lead role in its politics. It was the House's answer to and a tweaked version of Senate bill 744, which Republican House leaders had refused to take up. The House version replaced some of the provisions contained in the Senate bill, primarily those having to do with border security, with some they believed would be more acceptable to Republicans. It retained the entrepreneur visas contained in the Senate version. Still, it didn't get very far. While it was hoped to be a good compromise, the politics of the day simply didn't favor comprehensive immigration reform.

Senate vs. House:

A comparison of the provisions in the Senate and House Startup visa bills shows in essence that the Senate bill would be more successfully applied. Why does it matter now since none of these bills seem destined to become law?

It demonstrates real opportunities for passing a Startup Visa – and the colossal failings on the part of Congress each time. But more importantly, it shows that we have a foundation and language that we can build on for future bills.

The November 2014 mid-term elections resulted in the Democrats losing majority control of the Senate. It was a devastating blow for immigrants and their advocates, who read this as an end of any opportunity, at least in the near-term, for compromise on immigration. Now, with both Senate and the House now controlled by the Republican Party, whose platform and policies traditionally are more geared toward immigration enforcement and border security than to any creative response to our immigration problems, it is unlikely we will see any real progress regarding reform in the near future. But there could be the possibility of smaller, piecemeal legislation, like the ones we've discussed here.

Changes Without Congress

R hetoric and red-tape. Both are hindering immigration policies that could benefit entrepreneurs. As Former New York Mayor Michael Bloomberg stated, "[o]ur nation cannot afford to wait for Washington to get its act together and pass comprehensive immigration reform. There is too much at stake. Our economy demands that we take immediate action on the most urgent – and politically attainable – reform: making it easier for job creators to come and stay here."[37]

While Congress remains stalled, much can be done through policy changes to reach interim solutions. To that end, November 20, 2014, was a historic day in U.S. immigration history. President Obama, citing the failure of Congress to act, announced a series of executive actions – putting an end to the rhetoric and making a good faith and brave effort to include entrepreneurs in this executive action plan.

While he cannot create the new Startup Visa without Congressional approval – and his actions now can be undone with the swipe of the next president's pen later – Obama was creative in his solution. Using something known as the "significant public benefit" prong contained in existing laws, he proposed a new program called entrepreneurial parole. Researchers, inventors and co-founders of startup companies, who have raised money from U.S. investors and created or have the potential to create jobs, will be allowed to enter the U.S. on a case-by-case basis. This is an inventive solution for entrepreneurs who otherwise would not be permitted to enter the U.S. My client, Simon Smith, can take advantage of this as soon as it is implemented. He lives in London, UK and is one of four co-founders of a technology startup. The other three are U.S. citizens. Simon has worked remotely from his basement in London for over a year developing a software product. He didn't have any other, regular employment there during that time. A recent college graduate, he is unmarried and has no other significant ties to the UK. People like Simon cannot qualify for a B-1 Business Visa to stay in the U.S. for six months because they are unable to show significant familial or financial ties to their home countries and therefore cannot demonstrate intent to leave the U.S.

Citizens of the UK and select other countries, most in Europe, do not need a travel visa and may come to the U.S. as tourists, using passports issued by their own countries. But because of his lack of UK ties, Simon's entry as a visitor would likely raise suspicion at the airport and he could be subject to removal, affecting his chances to return in the future. Under entrepreneurial parole, he can come to the U.S. to be part of his team as it goes through a round of fundraising and continues to work on product development.

But while the entrepreneurial parole is a welcome option, it is not ideal for startup entrepreneurs for many reasons. Investors want stability of immigration status as they are generally investing more in people behind the product than the product itself. Parole is a discretionary vehicle for entering the country; there is no set timeline for how long a person may stay. Since the program will be administered on a case-by-case basis, there is room for arbitrary decisions. Therefore, I hope the administration takes these issues into consideration when establishing program guidelines.

Executive Action also addresses use of the National Interest Waiver (NIW) for entrepreneurs as discussed earlier, and it is expected that guidance will also be provided.

My hope is that we'll see measures that are reasonably achievable, similar to those contained in the Startup Act 3.0 or the Invest Visa provisions from the S.744 Senate immigration bill.

Another problem executive action is expected to address is the timing of when a green card application can be filed for those here on certain employment-based visas, such as H-1B and L-1. Such applications have various stages of intensely tedious steps to follow. The adjustment of status stage, or filing of the AOS petition, is the last step of this exhaustive process. Currently, it can only be filed once the person reaches the front of the line.[38] This so-called line, or the length of time one has to wait for a green card to become available for them, is in excess of 15 years for citizens of countries such as India and China. Executive action will establish a process to allow green card applications to be filed earlier so that applicants can receive work authorization sooner than they do now. Work authorization in this context is a kind of status that gives these workers flexibility to move from one employer to another. It will also give them the freedom to travel abroad more easily. The actual green card will be issued only when the person reaches the front of the line.

This policy change will also result in reinterpretation of a test known as 'same or similar' job test,[39] which is triggered when an applicant moves from one employer to another. Reinterpretation is necessary because this test is restrictive and does not adequately take into account career progression.

Why does this concern entrepreneurs? Currently, when visa workers reach the point where they can apply for green cards, they can use their aforementioned work authorization to become self-employed. The Partnership for a New American Economy released a report in 2011, called *Immigration and American Jobs*, which found a direct correlation between foreign-born workers with advanced STEM degrees from U.S. universities and the creation of American jobs.[40] This policy change alone will have a direct benefit to the U.S. economy.

Under the executive action plan, current visa options will be reviewed to make them more entrepreneur friendly, something I have been advocating for a long time. While it will be a few months before we know how all this will shake out, I have suggestions of what the administration might consider, based on my experience with clients over the years.

First, stop applying – at least to founders – the Neufeld Memo,[41] which requires proving employer/employee relationships for H-1B petitions. These entrepreneurs need to focus on operating their businesses and often will have many roles in addition to the one described under the terms of their H-1B visas. For example, as a business owner, I am not only a lawyer, but also a human resources manager, marketing manager, bookkeeper, and supervisor and perform countless other roles. To have my company control my job would impede my success.

Second, we should allow the use of cash substitutes, such as stock valuation, convertible notes, and other regularly used compensation methods instead of cash-only wages. Startups generally cannot afford high wages, particularly in the early stages. They need the opportunity to get their companies to the stage where they can be evaluated by investors for the funding. I understand the policy argument against cash substitutes may be fear of the entrepreneur becoming a public charge. But the USCIS should institute procedures to monitor and police that, revoking the visa of anyone who resorts to public assistance. This should apply to other visa categories for which startup founders might be eligible.

Third, modify current policies in various other visa categories to enable startup founders to obtain visas. For example, with some reinterpretation and policy changes, such options as E-2, TN and O-1 visas can be used for founders. For the E-2 treaty visa, I suggest the investment also include the value of intellectual property and other intangible assets, since startup founders do not often have a lot of money but have rich minds and valuable intellectual property.

While TN visa holders are generally not allowed to be self-employed, the written law does not actually prevent it. Yet anyone who shows up at the border, presenting a TN visa for self-employment in the U.S., is sure to get a swift denial.

There needs to be guidance from the Department of Homeland Security to all its agencies so that adjudication across the board is consistent. Many Canadians could actually come to the U.S. and start their companies if ownership interests are not treated as a death knell to the TN application.

And finally, we should allow the USCIS to recognize modern business practices which include the use of home offices, virtual offices and incubators as legitimate work places, particularly in the H-1B and L-1 context. In the world of modern technology, one only needs a laptop, a printer and phone to conduct a successful business.

There are many examples of such successes. Facebook got its start in a university dorm room. Yet the USCIS typically views home offices or virtual offices with suspicion. Random site visits investigating fraudulent cases are common in H-1B cases and now extend to L visas, too. Extend them to cover these startup firms – whether they are operating from a garage, the basement of a home or a storefront – and accept them as legitimate and genuine work places. The way we do business has evolved; therefore policies need to change as well.

What else can be done without Congressional action? Flexibility within existing laws can be put to better use. For example, as mentioned before, H-1B visa holders employed at universities in the U.S. are not subject to the annual H-1B cap. That means universities can hire promising and talented graduates in appropriate university roles, while those graduates work simultaneously on their startups until they reach the point where they can qualify for self-employed H-1Bs.[42] It's already being done under what's called the Global Entrepreneur in Residence (GEIR) program. Implemented by the University of Massachusetts in Boston,[43] it is currently being considered for a national rollout under the leadership of an organization named Venture Politics.

It is commendable that President Obama is finally taking steps to address immigration policy as it relates to entrepreneurs. And USCIS should be credited for its EIR program, which allows a team of immigration officers, trained in cutting edge entrepreneurial issues, to work with startup firms, recognizing these firms and their founders have specific concerns that need careful consideration by experts. It seems to have worked well and incubators and shared work spaces have gained credibility through this program.

But immigration officers can only work within the parameters of policies that exist. It is these policies that need adjusting to match modern business practices. I believe the EIR program can be improved by updating USCIS policies to reflect this.

Conclusion

From pre-revolution Jamestown Settlement to present-day Silicon Valley, immigrants have had a hand in invention and innovation. From laying down railroad tracks to cutting-edge technology, they've helped to modernize the U.S. in every era.

Today, however, we are at an impasse in our immigration system that is blocking the next generation of inventors, innovators and entrepreneurs from bringing their ideas to the U.S. and preventing the ones already here as students or temporary workers from staying.

The idea of driver-less cars and the bionic eye are now within our grasp. But the potential for further, awe-inspiring advancements is beyond even our comprehension or imagination. As Vivek Wadhwa describes in a recent article, moon travel will be within reach for the everyday traveler, thanks to entrepreneurs.[44]

But not all those entrepreneurs are in the U.S. Innovative ideas are alive in the minds of people from countries all across the globe – from Mexico to Singapore, Pakistan to Romania to Canada.

Think of a country like India. What were once the slums of Bombay are producing some of today's boldest innovators. Countries like

India are becoming technology hubs, with U.S.-educated Indian nationals returning home in droves to create new businesses, thanks to our restrictive immigration policies. But not just in India.

There was a time when technology was so costly, it was out of reach and off limits to the majority of Americans. And in distant parts of the world, people could only dream of linking to the Internet. But today, travel to any country, even some of the most remote parts of distant nations, and you see people walking about with cell phones – often smart phones – in hand, or sitting in coffee shops or public parks using tablets and laptops. Such accessibility has also made it easier for entrepreneurs to generate and implement their ideas, which in turn become the basis for startup firms. In some cases, they need little more than a computer and a telephone.

The truth is entrepreneurship can happen and is happening everywhere – on scales both small and large. To capture the vitality and economic growth foreign entrepreneurs and startups can bring, other countries rising out of the ashes of the last global financial crisis, are offering them a welcome embrace.[45] Yet, America remains a silent by-stander in this global competition. Today, the Chinese e-commerce company, Alibaba, is nipping at Amazon's heels. Tomorrow, who knows?

While this book has focused on the technology industry, the Startup Visa will apply to other sectors, too. Entrepreneurs and small business owners – from Main Street to Wall Street – are the backbone of the U.S. economy. Nevertheless, it is the technology revolution and global competition that are fueling this urgent need.

As Eric Lui, senior law lecturer at University of Washington and CEO of Citizen University, which works to help Americans build a culture of citizenship, stated, "the U.S. is an incubator for the world where ideas are spread around the planet."[46] For the U.S. to continue to spread ideas, to remain globally competitive, to bring talent to our shores, our immigration laws must change. And in a constantly evolving and ever-shrinking global economy, creation of the Startup Visa should not even be in question.

Endnotes

1 Vivek Wadhwa is a fellow at Rock Center for Corporate Governance at Stanford University, director of research at Center for Entrepreneurship and Research Commercialization at Duke, and distinguished fellow at Singularity University.

2 Vivek Wadhwa, How Today's Technology is Rapidly Catching Up to Star Trek, *The Washington Post*, July 1, 2014

3 The other co-sponsors are Sens. Coons, D-Del., Blunt R-Mo., Kaine, D-Va. and Klobuchar D-Minn. A summary of the provisions can be found at this link http://www.moran.senate.gov/public/index.cfm/files/serve?File_id=f6654812-2a6f-4826-8379-186d6580dab8.

4 Tim Kane, *The Importance of Startups in Job Creation and Job Destruction*, Ewing Marion Kauffman Foundation, July 2010.

5 Ibid.

6 Dane Stangler and Jared Konczal, *Give Me Your Entrepreneurs, Your Innovators: Estimating the Employment Impact of a Startup Visa*, Ewing Marion Kauffman Foundation, February 2013.

7 Debojyoti Ghosh, Deepti Chaudhary, Sohini Mitter, India's E-Tail Battleground: Amazon, Flipkart and Snapdeal Fight for Top Slot, *Forbes* India, June 24, 2014.

8 Stuart Anderson, *Immigrant Founders and Key Personnel in America's 50 Top Venture-Funded Companies*, National Foundation for American Policy, December 2011

9 Dane Stranger and Jason Weins, *The Economic Case for Welcoming Immigrant Entrepreneurs*, Kauffman Foundation, March 31, 2014. http://www.kauffman.org/what-we-do/resources/entrepreneurship-policy-digest/the-economic-case-for-welcoming-immigrant-entrepreneurs

10 https://www.pg.com/en_US/downloads/media/Fact_Sheets_CompanyHistory.pdf

11 http://cprr.org/Museum/Chinese.html

12 http://immigration.about.com/od/successfulimmigrants/p/LeviStrauss.htm

13 http://www.levistrauss.com/investors/annual-reports/2013-annual-report/

14 http://www.uscis.gov/tools/glossary/country-limit

15 http://encyclopedia.densho.org/Immigration_Act_of_1952/

16 http://www.forbes.com/companies/bose/

17 http://www.google.com/about/company/history/

18 https://investor.google.com/corporate/faq.html; https://investor.yahoo.net/faq.cfm; http://www.wsj.com/articles/SB10001424052970203888070457808 6791883555854

19 Tight immigration rules divert high tech brains from Seattle to Santiago, PSB Newshour, October 19, 2013. http://www.pbs.org/newshour/bb/science-july-dec13-chileconvalley_10-19/

20 Shane Phelan, Low take-up in visa scheme to attract wealthy foreigners, Independent.ie, May 26, 2014. http://www.independent.ie/irish-news/low-takeup-in-visa-scheme-to-attract-wealthy-foreigners-30304386.html

21 Vivek Wadhwa, Snapdeal- The flourishing company America passed on- offers a lesson about immigration reform, *The Washington Post*, November 7, 2014.

22 Ben Forer and Christine Brouwer, Immigrant Entrepreneur Gets Visa After 'World News' Story, ABC News, November 2, 2011.

23 https://iiusa.org/blog/research-analysis/iiusacommissioned-2012-eb5-economic-impact-report-set-publication-week/

24 Canada and Quebec Announce New Investor Programs For Canadian Immigration, Canadian Immigration Newsletter, December 2014.

25 Treaty Country List can be found on the Department of State website: http://travel.state.gov/content/visas/english/fees/treaty.html

26 8 CFR §214.2(e)(14)

27 Questions & Answers: USCIS Issues Guidance Memorandum on Establishing the "Employee-Employer Relationship" in H-1B Petitions, August 2011. http://www.uscis.gov/news/public-releases-topic/business-immigration/questions-answersuscis-issues-guidance-memorandum-establishing-employee-employer-relationship-h-1b-petitions

28 8 CFR §214.2(h)(8)(ii)(B).

29 DHS Memorandum, Implementation of L-1 Visa Regulations, August 9, 2013. http://www.oig.dhs.gov/assets/Mgmt/2013/OIG_13-107_Aug13.pdf

30 http://www.uscis.gov/news/public-releases-topic/business-immigration/employment-based-secondpreferenceimmigrant-visa-category-frequently-asked-questions-regarding-entrepreneurs-and-employment-based-second-preferenceimmigrant-visa-category

31 See Matter of New York State Department of Transportation, 22 I&N Dec. 215 (Comm'r 1998) ("NYSDOT").

32 USCIS Memorandum, Determining Employer-Employee Relationship for Adjudication of H1b Petitions, Including Third Party Site Placements, Donald Neufeld, January 8, 2010. http://www.uscis.gov/sites/default/files/USCIS/Laws/Memoranda/2010/H1B%20Employer-Employee%20Memo010810.pdf

33 As of January 2015, those with a Bachelor's degree from any country but India, China and Philippines must wait about 18 months; those from India with a Bachelor's degree must wait 12 years and Master's for 10 years, Chinese citizens with Bachelor's must wait just over 4 years and Master's just over 5 years and those from the Philippines must wait 18 months in both Bachelor's and Master's categories. However, these timeframes change frequently and people generally wait much longer than the timeframes listed. The Department of State releases a Visa Bulletin every month based on visas issued that determine the dates listed therein.

34 Entrepreneur in Residence, United States Citizenship and Immigration Services Initiative Summary, May 2013. http://www.uscis.gov/sites/default/files/USCIS/About%20Us/EIR/EntrepreneursinResidence.pdf

35 https://www.congress.gov/bill/113th-congress/house-bill/2131

36 Jennifer Martinez, Issa's tech-backed Skills Visa Act passes House Judiciary panel, The Hill, June 28, 2013.

37 Michael R. Bloomberg, A New Immigration Consensus, Wall Street Journal, May 2, 2011

38 USCIS Memorandum, Interim Guidance for Processing Form I-140 Employment-Based Immigrant Petitions and Form I-485 and H-1B Petitions Affected by the American Competitiveness in the Twenty-First Century Act of 2000 (AC21) (Public Law 106-313), William Yates, May 12, 2005.

39 http://www.uscis.gov/news/questions-and-answers/questions-about-same-or-similar-occupational-classifications-under-american-competitiveness-twenty-first-century-act-2000-ac21

40 http://www.renewoureconomy.org/wp-content/uploads/2011/12/NAE_Im-AmerJobs.pdf

41 USCIS Memorandum, Determining Employer-Employee Relationship for Adjudication of H1b Petitions, Including Third Party Site Placements, Donald Neufeld, January 8, 2010.

42 Immigrant Entrepreneurs: A Path To U.S. Economic Growth, Kauffman Foundation, January 22, 2015

43 Sara Ashley O'Brien, Can States Solve the Immigration Crisis, CNN Money, September 29, 2014.

44 Vivek Wadhwa, With innovators from around the globe digging in, moon travel may be only 20 years away, VentureBeat, January 2, 2015

45 Immigrant Entrepreneurs: A Path to Economic Growth, Kauffman Foundation, January 22, 2015. The report discusses samples of Startup Visas in other countries.

46 Eric Lui made the comment at a live event held at University of Washington School of Law "Race, Immigration and Citizenship," January 14th 2015. He is also the author of The Accidental Asian: Notes of a Native Speaker.

About the Author

Tahmina Watson, founder of Watson Immigration Law, is an experienced immigration attorney with a practice exclusively in the area of U.S. immigration law. An immigrant entrepreneur with more than 10 years' experience – eight of them spent navigating the U.S. immigration system on behalf of clients – Tahmina's unique perspective and pro-active approach are a breath of fresh air for her roster of clients, who include foreign workers, international entrepreneurs, investors and businesses. She regularly assists them with all types of employment-based immigration including L-1, E-2, H-1B, O-1, EB-1 and EB-5 visas and National Interest Waivers.

Tahmina rose quickly to become a leading authority on the Startup Visa, maintaining a highly interactive blog that boasts more than 700 subscribers and 10,000 unique viewers monthly. Her innovative message of pro-business immigration reform has been referenced in a study about entrepreneurship by the Competitive Enterprise Institute, and featured on KOMO4, KING5, as well as the glossy magazines and the web portals of *The Seattle Times*, *Puget Sound*

Business Journal, CNN Money, *Bloomberg Business Week*, NPR, GeekWire and *Entrepreneur Magazine*. A leader in her field, Tahmina is an active member of the American Immigration Lawyers Association, as well as other local and national associations and is a past president of the King County Washington Women Lawyers.

Born in London, England and of Bangladeshi descent, Tahmina obtained her law degree from Brunel University in London. A member of the Honorable Society of the Middle Temple, she attended the Inns of Court School of Law to become a barrister. After practicing in London for a short while, she immigrated to the U.S., where she is also a citizen. Admitted into the New York State Bar in 2006, Tahmina practices in Seattle, Washington, where she lives with her husband and two daughters. She is fluent in English, Bengali, Urdu, and Hindi.

Index

A

AILA 6
American Bar Association 28
American Immigration Lawyers Association 6, 70
angel investor 26, 53, 54

B

Border Security, Economic Opportunity and Immigration Modernization Act 51
Border Security, Economic Opportunity, and Immigration Modernization Act of
     2013 55
Brazil 3, 13, 26, 28

C

Canada 3, 13, 25, 26, 30, 63
China 3, 20, 28, 31, 36
Chinese Exclusion Act of 1882 19
Chris Coons, D-Del. 50

D

Donald Neufeld 39

E

E-2 30, 31, 53, 55, 61, 69
E-2 Treaty Investor Visa 30
EB-1 35, 69
EB-1 Extraordinary Ability 35
EB-5 29, 30, 31, 49, 69

EB-5 Investor Visa 29
EB-5 visa program 30
EB-6 49
EB-8 53, 54
EIR 44, 45, 62, 68
Entrepreneur in Residence (EIR) 44
Entrepreneur Visa 50, 53, 54
Ewing Marion Kauffman Foundation 6, 13

G

Germany 19, 27
Global Entrepreneur in Residence (GEIR) 62
Google 22, 29, 30, 37
Go UK 27

H

H-1B 31, 32, 33, 35, 36, 39, 40, 41, 42, 43, 60, 61, 62, 68, 69
H-1B Benefit Fraud and Compliance Assessment 39
House Judiciary Committee 53
H.R.15 55
H.R. 2131 53

I

IIRIRA 22
Illegal Immigration Reform and Immigrant Responsibility Act 22
immigrant entrepreneurs 3, 9, 14
Immigration Act of 1924 20
Immigration Act of 1990 21
Immigration and American Jobs 60
Immigration and Nationality Act of 1952 20
Immigration and Nationality Act of 1965 20
Immigration Reform and Control Act (IRCA) 21
India 3, 13, 20, 21, 28, 31, 36, 63, 64
Invest Visa 51, 52, 59
IRCA 21
Ireland 27
Italy 13, 27

J

John Kerry, D-Mass. 49
Judiciary Committee 49, 50, 53

K

Kunal Bahl 13

L

L-1 33, 34, 61, 69
L-1 Intra-Company Transferee 33
Levi Strauss 19

M

Mark Warner, D-Va. 50
Michael Bloomberg 28, 57
Microsoft 29, 42, 43

N

National Interest Waiver 35, 59
Neufeld Memo 39, 40, 60
New Zealand 27

O

O-1 Extraordinary Ability 34
O-1 visa 34

P

Pakistan 63
Partnership for a New American Economy 22, 28, 60
Proctor & Gamble 18

R

Rep. Darrell Issa, R-Calif. 53
Rep. Joe Garcia, D-Fla. 55
Rep. Zoe Lofgren, D-Calif 53
Richard Lugar, R-Ind. 49
Romania 63
Roy Blunt, R-Mo. 50

S

S. 310 50
S. 565 50
S. 744 51, 52, 53
S. 3029 49

43430111R00051

Made in the USA
Lexington, KY
28 June 2019